Bilingual Edition
READING POWER
Edición Bilingüe

School Activities

Community Service

Servicio comunitario

Rae Emmer

The Rosen Publishing Group's
PowerKids Press™ & Buenas Letras™
New York

Published in 2003 by The Rosen Publishing Group, Inc.
29 East 21st Street, New York, NY 10010
Copyright © 2003 by The Rosen Publishing Group, Inc.

First Bilingual Edition 2003
First Edition in English 2002

Book Design: Christopher Logan
Photo Credits: Maura Boruchow

Thanks to Westtown School
Gracias a la Escuela Westtown

Emmer, Rae
Community Service/Servicio Comunitario/Rae Emmer; traducción al español: Spanish Educational Publishing
p. cm. — (School Activities)
Includes bibliographical references and index.
ISBN 0-8239-6900-2 (lib. bdg.)
1. Student Service—Juvenile literature. 2. Beaches—Juvenile literature[1. Beaches—Juvenile literature. 2. Spanish Language Materials—Bilingual.] I. Title. II.School activities (New York, N.Y.)

Printed in The United States of America

Contents

Contenido

It is Earth Day.
We want to help our planet.

Es el Día de la Tierra.
Queremos ayudar
a nuestro planeta.

We are getting in the school van. We are going on a trip to clean the beach.

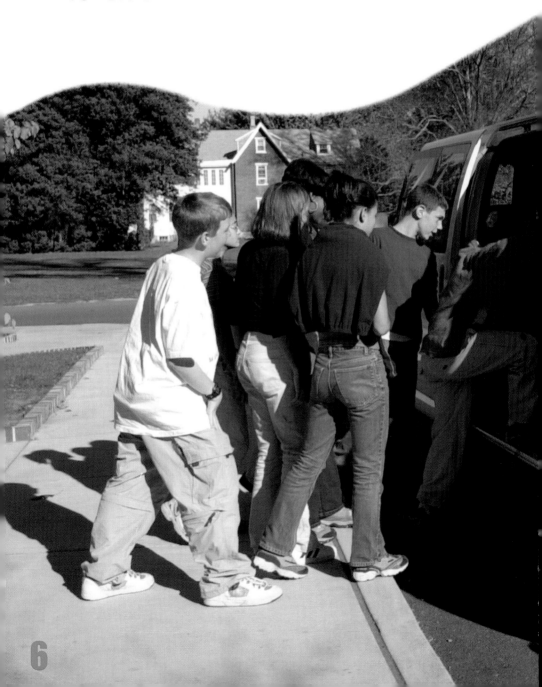

Nos subimos
a la camioneta escolar.
Vamos a limpiar la playa.

We get bags. We get gloves
to keep our hands clean.

———————————

Tenemos bolsas.
Nos ponemos guantes
para no ensuciarnos las manos.

We find bottles, cans, and papers.

Encontramos botellas, latas y papeles.

We put bottles in this bag.

Ponemos las botellas
en una bolsa.

We put cans in this bag.

———————————

Ponemos las latas
en otra bolsa.

We put papers in this bag.

Ponemos los papeles
en otra bolsa.

We will take the bags to the recycling center.

Llevamos las bolsas
al centro de reciclaje.

The beach is clean now.
We like to help.

———————————————

Ahora la playa está limpia.
Nos gusta ayudar.

Glossary

Earth Day (erth day) a day set aside to honor the planet

planet (**plan**-iht) one of the nine large objects that move around the sun

recycling center (ree-**sy**-klihng **sehn**-tuhr) a place where things are treated so they can be used again

Glosario

centro de reciclaje (el) lugar donde se transforman las cosas para poder usarlas de nuevo

Día de la Tierra (el) día especial para acordarse de cuidar el planeta

planeta (el) uno de los nueve objetos grandes que giran alrededor del Sol

Resources / Recursos

Here are more books to read about community service:
Otros libros que puedes leer sobre servicio comunitario:

How We Made Our World a Better Place
by The Fairview Press Staff
Fairview Press (1998)

The Kids' Volunteering Book
by Arlene Erlbach
Lerner Publishing Group (1998)

Web sites
Due to the changing nature of Internet links, PowerKids Press has developed an online list of Web sites related to the subject of this book. This site is updated regularly. Please use this link to access the list:

Sitios web
Debido a las constantes modificaciones en los sitios de Internet, PowerKids Press ha desarrollado una guía on-line de sitios relacionados al tema de este libro. Nuestro sitio web se actualiza constantemente. Por favor utiliza la siguiente dirección para consultar la lista:

http://www.buenasletraslinks.com/chl/tmb

Word count in English: 80
Número de palabras en español: 70

Index

B

bag, 8, 12, 14,
    16, 18
beach, 6, 20
bottles, 10, 12

C

cans, 10, 14

E

Earth Day, 4

G

gloves, 8

P

papers, 10, 16
planet, 4

R

recycling center, 18

Índice

B

bolsa, 8, 12, 14,
    16, 18
botellas, 10, 12

C

centro de reciclaje, 18

D

Día de la Tierra, 5

G

guantes, 8

L

latas, 10, 14

P

papeles, 10, 16
planeta, 4
playa, 7, 20